FOREST ORPHANS

BY AUGUST DERLETH

Sincerely, August Derleth

Edward Ernest, inc.

Publisher • New York

For Cherie
from
The Harold Nelsons

Contents

Carl Marty with three animal friends: fox, dog, and skunk.

Foreword

"If man will come ten percent of the way, the animal will come ninety percent." Motivated by this conviction, Carl Marty has made friends with scores of animals at his home in the heart of the wilderness near Three Lakes, Wisconsin—not caged animals, but wilderness dwellers whose association with him is wholly of their own choosing, since they come out of the forest and return to it at will. Foxes, bears, raccoons, muskrats, otters, beavers, deer, skunks, porcupines—whatever dwells in the area is Carl Marty's neighbor and friend in a unique relationship which, Carl Marty maintains, is possible for anyone who is not at heart inimical to animals.

Carl Marty has become a legend in his lifetime because of his friendship for animals. The great and the humble come to his wilderness to see for themselves indisputable evidence of the rightness of what he believes—the natural friendliness of wilderness creatures large and small—and proof that animals look upon him as a fellow-animal. No greater compliment could be paid Carl Marty.

A Northernaire villa.

I. The Unaware Years

CARL MARTY was born at the turn of the century in Monroe, Wisconsin, the heart of the dairy country, but in his first year moved with his parents sixteen miles to the east, to the village of Brodhead. The village took its name from an official of the Milwaukee Railroad when it was pushed through the region over four decades before, on its way to Madison from Janesville. Brodhead itself was not on the main line, but on the spur from Janesville to Mineral Point.

Carl was one of seven children; he had two brothers and four sisters. His

A winter scene in the woods near the Northernaire.

father, the senior Carl Marty, had come to America from Switzerland at the age of thirteen and gone to work in a cheese factory in Monroe. He left it briefly at eighteen to take a business course in Milwaukee, and for several years he edited the Green County *Herold,* a German-language newspaper, but after his marriage he went to work for the Brodhead Cheese and Cold Storage Company at a salary of thirteen dollars a week.

Brodhead was a rural village with a population of approximately 1200, and the Marty home had room for a large garden and a cow. The village stood on the site of a Winnebago Indian settlement; during the younger Carl Marty's childhood, corn hills were still to be found, and Indian mounds were both in and around the village. Brodhead lies in low, rolling country, agriculturally rich. Not far west of Brodhead the Sugar River winds its way, rising in the hills west of Madison and flowing into the Rock River south of Beloit. Carl's earliest memories, apart from those of his pleasant family life, are associated with this little river, at Brodhead hardly more than a broad brook.

From the time Carl was old enough to go along, he accompanied his father every Sunday on clamming expeditions in the Sugar River. The river

A brook in winter near the Northernaire.

was shallow and sandy, with segments of some depth and sudden deeps off the sandbars; clams abounded. It was Carl's task to complement his father's skilled hunting by carrying to shore the clams his father found, until a sizable mound of clams had accumulated. Both of them then set about opening the clams, with the expectation of discovering pearls of sufficient size to astonish jewelers. Although the sizable pearls were almost invariably imperfect, the two of them managed to accumulate enough well-proportioned small stones to enable the father to have rings made for his wife and daughters, each ring containing three pearls.

Clamming done and time permitting, father and son frequently explored the shores of the Sugar River in search of Indian artifacts, collecting flint arrowheads, stone axes, and occasional copper pieces. Indian occupation of the area had been sporadic, but over a long period of time, and there were an appreciable number of such artifacts to be found.

These Sunday excursions left an indelible impression on the boy and were his introduction to the world of nature. Here he grew to know the "kildee" of the kildeer, the rattling cries of kingfishers, the infinitely varied songs of frogs, the harsh "krark" of great blue herons, the pumping sounds of bitterns, the intimate talk of ducks, the "peet-weet" of solitary sandpipers—all of which were subsumed into his awareness and experience and taken, at his age, for a normal part of man's world. Here, as something forever intended for his pleasure, he heard the challenging cries of hawks on the wing and the voices of the flowing water and the wind in the maples lining the river —and giving it its name, for the sugar maples afforded many residents the opportunity to make maple sugar. He could not then know how his fellow men abused the kinship of the wild.

The years in Brodhead were idyllic, and Carl responded to the country-side with enthusiasm. He brought home one pet after another: rabbits, snakes, frogs, pigeons, guinea pigs; he was never without pets—not so much domestic animals as wild creatures brought in from the country. There is never any substitute for a childhood in the country, and in the relatively few years the Martys lived in Brodhead, Carl made the most of it.

When Carl was eight, his father was offered a position with the Glauser-Ladrick Company in Chicago; in 1907 the Martys left Brodhead and went to live on Wisconsin Street, near Clark, in the Chicago neighborhood now known as "Old Town," but then a middle-class, predominantly German area. Within that year Carl was selling newspapers at the corner of Wisconsin and Clark—a far cry from clamming and hunting Indian artifacts along the Sugar River.

But there were compensations. The Marty home was next door to Lincoln Park and the zoo, which was then under the direction of Cy DeVry, and Carl was drawn there repeatedly, even though the caged animals, however fascinating, were an inadequate substitute for the wild things he had known. It was not long before he caught DeVry's attention and was invited to join that select circle of youngsters who were permitted to pet the lion cubs and to know other animals on more intimate terms than cages customarily allowed. This was an extension of his experience at Brodhead, and he found the knowledge of animals without the intervention of bars infinitely more pleasing than the simple viewing of the caged beasts.

Attractive as it was, however, the zoo was only the reward Carl gave himself when he was not in school or at work. For, as early as ten years of age, Carl was buying cheese from his father's company, importing honey in five-gallon tins from Wisconsin, and taking it around to the rooming houses in his area of the city to sell it at a profit. Early in life he had been imbued

A badger, after whom the Badger State is named.

After seeing Carl Marty and Ginger, the badger has decided to come out of the woods.

by his father with the importance of the security one's own earnings afforded and, even more, of the necessity of work in every man's life. The Germans who came to America held to an old adage—"Arbeit macht das Laben süsz" ("Work sweetens life")—and the senior Carl Marty lived by it.

Carl's enterprise blossomed in the summer months. By the time he was twelve, he had considerably expanded his selling activities by adding to cheese and honey the sale of fresh fruit and vegetables. In the early part of the century there were no neighborhood fresh produce stores; the central farmers' markets were many miles from most city neighborhoods, which were served by produce wagons. In the vicinity of Wisconsin and Clark, people bought their fresh fruit and vegetables from a local seller who hawked them up and down the streets and was known to one and all as John the Greek. Greeks, as a matter of fact, did most of the produce business in Chicago at that time; as Carl remembers it, "They owned the fattest horses, the finest, most polished harnesses, and beautifully painted wagons, often very colorful, along the sides of which their names frequently appeared in gold leaf—or what looked like gold leaf."

With the expansion of trade in his corner of the city, John the Greek had to add a second wagon which, like most second wagons, was not quite as flamboyantly painted as the first. The second wagon seldom carried produce of the first quality, but was loaded with second-grade fruit and vegetables and such first-grade produce as was overly ripe and had not sold the day before or was still too green. This second wagon was Carl's to drive; he was sent out with instructions to sell the produce on it at the best possible price, but at no time and in no circumstance to bring anything back at the end of the day. He was given no salary but worked solely on a commission of fifteen percent. At this commission he usually earned at least a dollar a day; if he earned as much as a dollar and a half, he considered that he had had a good day indeed.

This new task meant long hours. John the Greek lived two miles from the Marty home. His work required Carl to leave home by 4:30 in the morning; by the time he had walked to his employer's place and picked out the second-grade fruit he had to sell, the hour would be close to six, after which he had a drive of from one to one and a half hours to reach the neighborhood he had been assigned to cover. This was only the beginning of a day, the length of which depended upon his success in selling his pro-

16

The pine marten—a little animal which received no protection until almost extinct.

WALLACE KIRKLAND

duce, and it was seldom that his day ended before nightfall.

Sometimes his day extended very late, although if his fruit and vegetables had sold well he could reduce his price and sell the remainder at the end of the day to his mother or some other special customer. Then, when the produce wagon was empty, he took the horse and wagon back to the stable, rubbed down the horse, and walked the two miles back to his home to rest before the next day's tasks. This work took up his summers while he attended LaSalle Grammar School, from which he graduated when he was fourteen.

A half-year business course at Waller High School followed. A full high-school education was not considered a necessity in the years before the First World War, particularly not for an ambitious young fellow who intended to go into business, as Carl did. On the completion of his course, he went to work in the business he knew best—the cheese business—in his father's company at a starting salary of six dollars a week. In general, he intended to follow the career his father had cut out for himself and at which he had been successful enough to show every promise of achieving his goal of retirement by the age of fifty.

World War I interrupted Carl's plans. Like many another young man,

Four Mile Lake looking east.

Carl volunteered for service in the U. S. Marines, never thinking that the war might bring about many changes affecting his future. One of those changes was the liquidation of the business for which he had worked and which his father had owned since 1915. So, after fifteen years in Chicago, during which the senior Marty had moved steadily up the ladder from employee to partner and then sole owner, the Marty family returned to Wisconsin, where in 1922 Carl, now married to Margaret Dietz of St. Louis, started his own cheese business in Monroe. He specialized in Swiss cheese, under the name of Carl Marty and Company.

Monroe is the center of Wisconsin's dairy country, and the business flourished. Before very many years had passed. Carl's brother Robert became associated with the company, and at the same time—in the late 1920's—the company expanded by purchasing the Borden's Condensed Milk plant at Monroe. Not long afterward, Carl headed a group of men organized to buy the Blumer Brewery at Monroe, which had been offered for sale as a result of Prohibition, and developed it into a cold storage warehouse.

Despite a mild recession in the post-war years, the expanding business was so successful as to attract the attention of the Borden Company, which

negotiated for the purchase, in 1939, of Carl Marty & Company. Although the formation of the Capital Cheese Company was not far from reality, Carl was now free to satisfy a long-burgeoning desire to strike out for northern Wisconsin, specifically the Three Lakes area.

The Three Lakes country, then virtually wilderness, a region of many lakes with forests surrounding the settlements, was not strange to him. In 1915 his father had purchased some lakeside property not far from the village of Three Lakes and in the following year had built a cottage on it. Carl himself seldom spent any time there, apart from weekends, because of the pressure of his work, but the Three Lakes cottage was a haven for the family for many years, while the general area began to develop, particularly with the establishment of a community golf course not far from the Marty property.

The golf course, however, languished after a promising start in spite of its location in the heart of beautiful lake country which offered golfers admirable landscapes in every direction from the course and vistas of forest and lake abounding in wild life. The Marty brothers, concluding that what the venture needed was a clubhouse, had for some time considered buying the

19

A visiting raccoon.

property; the sale of Carl Marty & Company to the Borden Company made that purchase possible, and without delay the brothers bought the golf course and began the construction of a clubhouse, which opened in 1940. With their business interests now divided between Monroe and Three Lakes, the brothers wisely decided to divide the control—Robert to take over the business in Monroe, Carl to develop the Three Lakes property.

That development came to full flower seven years later when, on July 1, the Northernaire, a handsome modern resort hotel, was opened on the lake shore between the clubhouse and the Marty cabin. The clubhouse, renamed the Showboat, which it resembled in structure, had been converted into a quasi nightclub, with entertainment every evening—dancing, miming,

20

sleight of hand, and the like. The Northernaire was in every way a challenge to Carl Marty's ingenuity, for it had been established in a relatively new resort area, on the very edge of the wilderness. Carl was prepared to meet the challenge.

But the Northernaire and its development were not to be his greatest adventure.

A badger and an otter together
in the woods near the Northernaire.

Bernese, the St. Bernard, playing with fox and fawn friends.

2. The Lesson of the Fox
and the Dog

LONG AGO the rapacious lumber barons cut down the original forests of
northern Wisconsin. The area around the Northernaire was typical: there
were scattered old trees and occasional stands of virgin forest, but for the
most part it was a new growth of trees that crowded up to the shores of all
the lakes and to the very edge of the cleared area where the Northernaire
rose. Pines alternated with deciduous trees to make a very pleasing prospect.
For years the senior Carl Marty enthusiastically celebrated this country on

canvas and in print. His poems were in German and in English, and a bi-lingual collection of them published in 1922 contained several tributes to the country around Three Lakes:

> . . . *enter nature's holy shrines,*
> *Rest on its balmy peaceful shores,*
> *And listen to the whispering pines.*

It was indeed country to move a man to verse, a country in which were native the black bear, porcupine, beaver, badger, fox, otter, mink, wolf, deer, raccoon, and many another wilderness dweller; loons cried from the lakes, herons abounded, hawks and eagles dominated the skies; in May trilliums overspread its woodland areas and yellow and orange hawkweed set its land-scapes aflame in June. Native Indians were not infrequently found in this still rather sparsely settled area not far from the Michigan peninsula and Lake Superior. Lakes and waterways were so plentiful and so interrelated in the area that the natives of the Three Lakes country boasted that it was possible to travel around the world by water from Three Lakes.

Ginger guards a ten-week-old fox.

It was here that Carl Marty stumbled upon a new awareness of animals—an awareness and a knowledge that enriched him beyond anything he might have expected. His experience began late one night, after midnight. The Northernaire had not yet been built, and Carl was walking to his cabin from the clubhouse with his cocker spaniel, Rusty, who had run on ahead of him. Carl, being tired, followed at a more leisurely pace. He was almost at the cabin when he saw Rusty ahead of him—Rusty and another animal.

He went more slowly and finally stood still in amazement. The other animal was a red fox. Instead of the fox taking flight with Rusty at its heels, the two animals, domestic and wild, were playing with each other. Incredible as it was, Rusty and the fox were playing as two dogs might play, making short runs at each other, tumbling together, and rolling on the ground, all to the accompaniment of mock growls and eager whining. This sight was so alien to Carl's experience and to all he had understood about the natural enmity between domestic and wild animals that he was astonished by this evidence to the contrary. He watched the scene until he was impelled to move forward to learn what the fox would do. But the fox hesitated only a few moments at his approach, then turned and vanished into the woods.

What he had seen was unique in Carl Marty's experience. Wild and domestic animals playing together is not a rare occurance, but witnessing it for the first time disabused Carl of certain concepts about animals he had held since childhood. At the same time it renewed his childhood interest in wild animals that had been all but dormant during the Chicago years and the decade after.

If a fox could befriend a dog, why not a man?

Knowing that he might have to wait endlessly for another fox to come out of the woods, Carl had a young fox brought to him and vowed to tame it so that when the time came to release it, the animal would return. The young fox proved to be a graceful and intelligent companion for Rusty. Like the dog, he was allowed to roam unconfined in the house and was readily trained.

When at last the time for release came, Carl cut a small in the screen door of the porch. The fox presently found it, stuck his head through it, and pulled back. Next time he got half his body through before he came back into the house. But at last he went all the way through, walked a short distance from the house, and returned. Having at last gone so far, he made a

Ginger with 3 four-week-old foxes.

*Rusty with a litter of
four gray foxes.*

game of going in and out of the house, racing around it several times before coming back in. But at last he vanished under the house.

Was he gone? Carl and his family wondered.

For two hours nothing was heard of the fox. Then he reappeared and stood scratching at the living-room door. He had been so well trained that it had not occurred to him that he need not come into the house to relieve himself.

Next the fox ventured into the nearby woods but always came back to spend his nights under the house, bedding down in clothing he picked up and carried out of the house. But however well he was adapting to life in the wilderness, he invariably responded to Carl's call.

The fox was accustomed to Carl, his wife, and their son Michael. Would his pattern of trust extend to other human beings as well? As soon as an opportunity presented itself, Carl brought guests to the cabin and called the fox once, twice, and again—and within two minutes the fox came out of the woods directly to where Carl and his guests stood, showing no hesitation in the presence of other human beings. The pattern of trust had apparently

*Rusty watches a fawn and a fox eat
by the fireplace at Bear Point.*

been established not only with Carl, but with any human being associated with him.

After calling Rusty, Carl and his guests watched fox and dog at their mock fighting, the fox demonstrating fighting tactics clearly superior to those of the dog, for Rusty was slow compared to the fox. Within minutes the fox had Rusty by the throat. In actual battle, the fox would have torn the dog's throat out; in play the fox simply relaxed his hold, and the game would begin all over again.

In all his actions, the fox was completely spontaneous. Nothing had been required of him beyond elementary house-training; the indignity of tricks had never been levied upon him, and in time he had also become thoroughly adjusted to the wilderness which was his heritage. The only confinement he had ever known was that of the house when he was very young, and he had had the freedom to roam about the house as much as he liked. The red fox has a well-merited reputation for being among the canniest of wild animals, filled with guile and cunning and extremely difficult to keep in captivity.

And he continued to come—as when he jumped through the open win-

27

Bernese looks after a six-week-old fox kit.

dow one night to sleep for a while at the foot of Carl's bed— until the time for his mating the following winter. Then he was seen no more. His failure to respond to calls at last convinced Carl that he had been trapped and killed, particularly when the time came for the new fox family to disband. At that point the fox would certainly have come back had he been free to do so, since the fox separates from the vixen when the family disbands in autumn and resumes his former solitary way of life until he finds a new mate or, as sometimes happens, returns to the old mate for another season.

Carl's experiment indicated that the fox—and by extension other animals —was not born with an innate fear of man. Caution, yes, but not fear. Gentleness, trust, and respect for the dignity of any animal could win its friendship. This initial experiment, of course, needed repetition.

Carl's next foxes were a pair of very young animals, weighing only a few ounces each when they were brought to him. Carl fed them on cow's milk at

A young red fox mirrored in the lake.

body temperature and then evaporated milk, and learned rapidly that the care of orphaned animals did not differ greatly from the care of human young. They needed warmth, yet not too much warmth, as their panting told him—for a panting animal is too warm and needs to be put into shade or removed from an over-heated room. They needed to be kept clean, too; Carl had to double for their lost mother by brushing their hair. As they lay under the brush, they whined their pleasure, the whine being the counterpart of a cat's purring. The young foxes exhibited no fear of other animals— neither of the household dogs, which the foxes and all other animals soon recognized as representatives of the master and learned to obey, nor of other young animals brought into the Marty's unique orphanage. Once weaned, the foxes' favorite food was chopped raw meat, but they also liked dog bisquits and cooked meat, in that order.

The two foxes, however, were lost at six months, and another fox was

29

Bernese in charge of five-week-old red fox orphans.

Bernese and a three-month-old fox getting to know one another.

brought to Carl. His experience with it repeated the already established pattern, although the new fox developed a great fondness for the cocker spaniel, Rusty, and after his liberation frequently came out of the woods to play with the dog.

The dog also sought the fox's company frequently, but Carl was not immediately aware of this. On nights when, preceded by Rusty, he walked over to the Showboat to play host, he was accustomed to notice Rusty vanish into the darkness and come into the Showboat later. Every time he opened the door for the dog, Carl was aware of some concern, almost distress, on the cocker's part, but did not understand it until one night when Rusty went out again. Looking out, Carl saw the fox sitting on its haunches at the edge of the light in front of the Showboat. Thereafter the two friends, dog and fox, regularly came up to the door and looked in. "It was as if they enjoyed the entertainment," said Carl. But the fox would not venture in; he was not afraid, simply unwilling to follow Rusty across the threshold. The Marty house was still within bounds; for one thing, it was surrounded by woods, whereas the Showboat was near the edge of the lake and in a sizable expanse of greensward, with little cover.

The success of Carl's experiments with foxes brought him other animals. The local game wardens, conservation department personnel, and people who had to surrender pets acquired during the vacation months—one after another they came to Carl's cabin in the woods with orphaned animals, loath to free them lest they be unfit to survive because they were too young. One and all, Carl took these forest orphans into his house and adopted them into his family. In the Three Lakes area the most commonly orphaned animals of the north woods are the fawns, some of them left motherless because the doe has been killed on the highway, some illegally picked up before they are able to run by travelers under the impression that the fawn has been abandoned.

For all their instant alertness and capacity for immediate flight when come upon in the forest, deer are readily domesticated, as Carl soon discovered after he had taken his first fawn into the cabin at the lake's edge. A deer is likely to retain less independence than a fox or any other wild creature, becoming attached to its source of food.

Carl's first deer was not a fawn, but a deer in its first year of life. She had been raised elsewhere and was brought to Carl when already accustomed to

Deer Lake, at the Northernaire.

ALLEN SCHULTZ

*This young buck, which came to the Northernaire four
days after his birth, is now an eight-point yearling.*

An orphan fawn in the woods near the Northernaire.

human companionship. In due time the doe brought her fawn to the cabin and became a familiar sight grazing on the lawn around the Northernaire, then under construction. At the beginning of the hunting season, doe and fawn were decorated with red ribbons. Unhappily, this did not save the doe's life. One day a quartet of archers drew up in their car; the trusting deer walked toward them and was shot from a distance of six feet. That these "sportsmen" were arrested by the game warden and fined was no comfort to Carl or to the workmen at the Northernaire.

Carl's second deer was also shot—soon after giving birth to twin fawns which Carl raised, bottle-feeding them as much as five quarts of milk a day. One of Carl's fawns developed rapidly into a handsome buck, fearless in satisfying his curiosity. During the construction of the Northernaire, the buck followed the workmen from place to place, even to the power saw, which had to be stopped frequently to spare his nose, and to the open stairs

A fawn less than half an hour old.

A doe with her newborn fawn, a few minutes old.

leading to the roof. But his favorite occupation at the Northernaire was to join the workmen at lunch time and beg for food. Even though the white-tailed deer is a selective feeder, the range of this buck's feeding was appreciably extended by the workmen at the Northernaire. Deer customarily eat a great many plants but seldom browse one spot, preferring to keep on the move; they will eat mushrooms, twigs, leaves, lichen, nuts, and occasional aquatic plants, but their curiosity about human beings extends also to the food men eat, a curiosity Carl was always interested in satisfying.

Another buck raised by Carl developed in one year into an eight-point buck, although deer at one year are supposed to be two-point bucks and hunters presume to tell a deer's age by its points. A deer fed largely on milk, like this buck at the Marty cabin, could very readily develop faster than its kin, which were limited to the fare offered by the forest.

Gentle as the deer invariably were, Carl had ample opportunity to become

The fawn with its head actually in Bernese's mouth.

Bernese, a fawn, and a beaver together.

*A porcupine with
Bernese and a fawn.*

familiar with their great strength, particularly on one occasion when he went with the wardens to help a buck trapped in the snow. It had held off seven wolves in spite of the fact that it had no antlers and was too deep in snow to use its hoofs effectively, but subsequently died of exhaustion.

Carl found, too, that while does returned after mating and brought their fawns when they were ready, bucks seldom returned, once liberated. Carl almost always knew where the does had their fawns; they chose some place not too far from the cabin—perhaps just across the neck of the lake from the Northernaire—but he never went to them, knowing the doe would select her own time to bring her young.

Deer are reputed to be secretive, and with good reason, for like most animals in the wild, deer are far more frequently aware of human beings in the forest than men are aware of their presence. Those at the Northernaire, once having known Carl's hospitality, proved anything but shy. Perhaps their keen hearing and their remarkable sense of smell told them there was little danger around the Northernaire. Like the foxes, the deer ventured out onto the lawns surrounding the Northernaire with the same feeling of security that the adjacent woods afforded them.

Occasionally neighborhood dogs pursued the deer, but the deer as frequently fought back. A deer's sharp hoofs and antlers are not to be regarded lightly, as such dogs eventually learned. But the major enemy of the deer at the Northernaire, as of deer elsewhere in Wisconsin, was always the hunter, legitimate as well as poacher, and more than one of Carl's deer fell victim to the hunting season, despite being plainly marked with red ribbons and reddened antlers. They were easy victims, since they had come to trust human beings and could not learn that men with guns were not quite the same as men without guns.

The slaughter of one of the beribboned deer in the same night that a friendly fox was wantonly slain impelled Carl to write an effectively bitter editorial for the *Three Lakes News* about the kind of hunter who could destroy a plainly-marked buck walking toward him in friendship. "There is a higher law he violated," he wrote of the hunter: "the law of sportsmanship and common decency. He and only he must live with his conscience." The editorial was not only widely reprinted in the Middle West but also broadcast on the radio by Arthur Godfrey and Paul Harvey, among others.

Perhaps more than anything else, the casual destruction of obviously friendly animals spurred Carl to take the first step toward some kind of counteraction. This was the establishment of the Three Lakes Wilderness Association, whose goal was the preservation and protection of wild life in an ever-widening area of northern Wisconsin.

DALE ROOKS

3. From an Affectionate Beaver to a Gentle Wolf

ALTHOUGH THE DEER, once his trust is won, is readily friendly and responds with eagerness to every overture from a human being, the beaver is not known for his response to men, who trap him and destroy his dams and colony houses. Infrequently seen by day, the beaver customarily emerges at sundown to cut willow, aspen, birch, or ash twigs—or other young trees if these favored ones are not available—and eat the bark for supper before busying himself for the night. Awareness of human beings almost invariably causes him to submerge, slapping the water vigorously with his flat tail as if to warn other beavers in the vicinity.

His damming activities often bring him afoul of human beings, and eventually the state conservation department is called upon to remove beavers from a given area because dammed-up water is spreading over fields, pastureland, or roadways.

After one such beaver family removal in the Three Lakes area, the state trappers found a tiny frightened beaver, overlooked in the evacuation of the colony and huddled in a far corner of the lodge. This young beaver, scarcely larger than Carl's fist, was brought to him by the trappers.

Carl was quick to accept the challenge of raising the beaver, without any illusions about the difficulty involved. Although he sought helpful information in various books, he found nothing useful. The diet and living habits of the beaver offer major problems; the animal prefers the bark and adjacent outer layers of such soft-barked trees as aspens, alders, osiers, willows, birches, and other similar trees, although it will also devour aquatic plants in some measure. Moreover, the beaver is peculiarly susceptible to pneumonia, particularly at an early age—a problem Carl met, on the chilly spring nights when the beaver had first been added to the Marty household, by simply encouraging him to sleep in bed nestled in the crook of Carl's arm with his paddle tail tucked under him. And there the young anmial stayed for its first two weeks in the house, while the weather warmed and the beaver grew.

The beaver's first food at Carl's hands was milk from a doll's nursing bottle. Carl had to persuade him to take this by first squirting the milk down his throat, after which the beaver learned to take the bottle himself. Later he progressed to bread and milk, then to apples and other foods. To his astonishment Carl found that one of the beaver's favorite foods was chopped beef—a preference that seemed to disprove the animal's reputation as a vegetarian. The beaver confirmed this preference later, when he was transferred to a trunk specially prepared for him in the animal house—a building Carl had constructed at the woods' edge for the use of any animals that wished to come from the forest to eat the food he left there for them. Among foods such as bread, apples, prunes, apricots, dates, grapes, plums, and chopped beef, the beaver was observed to devour the chopped beef before touching anything else. This feeding pattern proved invariable and was so unusual that state beaver experts had to observe the animal at its feeding before believing it themselves. There is no evidence of carnivorous feeding in the

Ginger and a beaver.

wild state, although there is some belief that beavers may eat clams on occasion. Carl's beaver also frequently ate as may as two apples, quartered,
holding the quarters in his forepaws in the typical manner of rodents.

The beaver grew rapidly and particularly attached to Carl. After eating
he sought out Carl and cried to be picked up, and after being picked up and
cradled in Carl's arms, he fell asleep. Carl's failure to respond at such times
would always upset the beaver, causing him to stand hugging Carl's leg
with his forepaws, whimpering and crying. Finally he would chew the door
and run about in a frenzy of irritation. Once the beaver had fallen asleep in
his arms, Carl could put him down, knowing that he would continue his nap.

In six months' time the beaver had grown stronger and sleeker than the
average wild beaver of his age. He had had access to the immediate lake
shore and beyond it to all the twenty-seven connected lakes—the complete
freedom all save the very young and comparatively helpless animals always
had in Carl's charge. Perhaps for lack of parental training, the beaver had
built his first home on the lakeshore with the entrance too near to the surface,
so that it froze, and he could not reach the food he had stored in the water—

Ginger waits while a young beaver drinks.

branches and twigs of his favorite trees bunched in one or more places in the water. These stores were reached from the beaver house by way of an underwater passage which enabled the beaver to swim under the ice to his food. Beavers make such economical use of oxygen that they can remain submerged for as long as a quarter of an hour and occasionally longer.

Before finding the lake, the beaver had become accustomed to the bathtub, where he enjoyed floating. There he swam every afternoon for an hour and then groomed himself, beginning with his abdomen and using the split nails on the second hind toes to comb his fur. Like all animals, he proved to be extremely clean and usually took half an hour daily for grooming.

Once completely free—after the spring ice breakup of his second year— he chose to build a summer house, a burrow in the lakeshore among the roots of an old pine about seven feet back from the edge of the lake. To this house he retired during most of the day, although he very often spent his nights in the trunk in the animal house. Carl had cut an opening into one end of the trunk, and the beaver had lined it with hay Carl had provided. Once in for the night, the beaver customarily closed the opening with the hay. He

43

kept his trunk home immaculate, but he was not averse to entertaining guests; on occasion he shared his bed with muskrats previously released by Carl and, like the beaver, accustomed to come to the animal house.

To the beaver, Carl was unquestionably the source of food, warmth and affection—the only parent he had. His response to Carl was filial: he came at Carl's special call for him, swimming in out of the lake if he was within hearing; he nuzzled Carl's legs and begged to be picked up; and he slept in perfect security in Carl's arms. On one occasion, two hours past midnight, when the beaver had been gone longer than his previous maximum of twelve hours, he deliberately attracted Carl's attention by slapping his tail three times on the water outside the Marty house where Carl sat reading, and uttering his characteristic beaver sounds—a sighing or mewing noise.

The beaver showed the same respect for everyone associated with Carl, even Ginger, Rusty's daughter. At first he tried—as with all other animals —to bluff the spaniel into accepting him as her superior in strength and fierceness. He advanced upon Ginger hissing pompously, then lunged at the dog and slapped the ground with his tail, but Ginger stood her ground. The

DALE ROOKS

*Irene Castle
and a beaver
at the lake.*

This beaver likes to be held by a human being.

Carl's beaver.

beaver then dropped and played dead, exactly like an opossum, and by this act tacitly acknowledged the dog's mastery of the situation. Once the beaver had acknowledged the dog's mastery, the two animals played together in perfect amity, although ultimately the beaver's assumption of full adult responsibilities in his world brought him back to Carl's less often. The dogs were generally accepted by the orphan animals as being in "control" or "speaking for" Carl; unlike the beaver, most of the animals saw no need to test the dogs' mettle. Of the two dogs, Rusty was naturally friendly to the animals and adopted them under his protection. Ginger, on the other hand, was trained to protect the animals coming out of the forest; and so, later, was the magnificent St. Bernard, Bernese, who came to the Northernaire in 1958 with Carl's second wife Loretta Sullivan, two years after the death of Carl's first wife.

The period in which the beaver was intimately associated with the Marty household was long enough for Carl to observe its friendship with bears, deer, raccoons, porcupines, and foxes, in addition to Ginger. In all these situations, however, the beaver and the other animals seemed anxious only to establish an amicable relationship, and in no case did fighting ever break out among them.

46

The beaver experience is perhaps unique, at the opposite pole from the experience of men with raccoons. The raccoon is one of the most pronounced extroverts in the wilderness—a genial, inquisitive little animal who speedily accustoms himself to any habitat and finds it easy to befriend human beings in spite of all the rapacity with which he is hunted by men. The raccoon is also one of the most attractive animals to be found in American woodland areas, with his appealing eyes, black facial mask, and searching paws. He is indigenous from coast to coast (except for a few mountain and desert areas) and both north and south of the border.

Carl's first raccoon was a little girl's pet. Unable to take him back to the city after her vacation in the north woods was over, she brought her pet, aptly named Snoopy, to Carl. Carl took Snoopy into the living room of his home and called Rusty, who approached the raccoon in his customary manner—slowly, wagging his tail—and stopped a foot away from the newcomer lest he startle him. But at this, Snoopy walked up to him immediately, they touched noses, and began a singularly fast friendship.

Their friendship was cemented next day when Snoopy, having crawled too far out on a limb that stretched over the lake, fell off into the water and Rusty, unaware that the raccoon could swim, jumped into the water and retrieved him. The two animals engaged in the usual mock fighting, at which Snoopy demonstrated the raccoon's superiority in many ways. Since

The beaver has lunch.

GATES PRIEST

Crying like a baby to be held.

the raccoon has a short neck and in fighting tends to hold his head low between his legs, he finds it easy to reach a dog's jugular vein without exposing his own.

One afternoon Carl witnessed an instance of what can only be described as an intelligence greater than is generally attributed to animals by mankind. Rusty and Carl were in the yard at the time, and Carl was too busy to open the door for Rusty to go back into the house, as the dog wished to do. The dog, impatient, turned and ran off into the woods. In a few minutes he returned with Snoopy at his heels. They went directly up to the screen door, where Rusty stepped aside for the raccoon. Snoopy opened the screen door with his flexible forepaws, Rusty went into the house, and the raccoon returned to the woods. Subsequently this became a commonplace: The dog used the raccooon to do what he himself could not do.

Snoopy had the run of the house. He made himself familiar with every corner of it without delay and quickly found the places where food of any kind was stored. Raccoons are notoriously fond of sweets, and his favorite food proved to be jelly roll. As soon as they discovered this, the Martys began to keep a supply of it in the lower storage drawer of the refrigerator, a place within easy reach of the raccoon. Snoopy enjoyed taking part in a game to get at his food, with Carl and his family pretending that the raccoon was not to touch the drawer and the raccoon persisting until finally he succeeded in getting to the jelly roll.

The beaver's introduction to the otters.

ROBERT H. MILLER, JR.

Snoopy also responded to the suggestion that he take his meals with the family now and then. He was put into a chair at the dining-room table, with the chair just far enough away from the table's edge to discourage him from climbing onto it. He sat there in his normal posture—on his hind legs—using his forepaws like hands, and ate each morsel of food as it was given him. Carl had long before learned that, contrary to another of the common bits of misinformation about animals, raccoons do not wash their food, but do wash their forepaws and sometimes their faces.

Snoopy willingly took part, too, in entertainments for guests at the Northernaire by responding to directions in what seemed to the credulous to be an extraordinarily intelligent way. Carl would blandly assure his audience that the raccoon could obey directions in eleven languages; he would ask a guest to decide whether the raccoon was to take a morsel of food with mouth or paws and to designate the language in which directions should be given. Snoopy never failed to respond, although it was a relatively simple deception. The raccoon, of course, did not understand a word of the directions, but simply reacted in accordance with his nature. If Carl held the food

The raccoon is interested in Carl and his fox, but the dog ignores him.

close enough, Snoopy took it with his mouth; if he held it even two inches farther away, the raccoon grasped it with his forepaws. Of course the raccoon was invariably an eager participant, tempted by the food; no animal at the Martys' was ever pressed into doing anything it did not wish to do.

In Snoopy's case, not even minimal protective confinement was necessary, for when he came to the Martys', the raccoon was no longer a baby in need of such protection. Snoopy could and did indulge his natural instinct to roam. His exposure to Carl Marty and his family and to the personnel and guests of the Northernaire heightened his natural friendliness to human beings. On occasion he wandered miles from home and was seen on the road-side by the game warden. Anxious to get back for food or for a mock battle with Rusty, which both the animals always enjoyed, he never hesitated to get into the warden's car for a ride home whenever the warden stopped for him.

Carl learned that the raccoon, like the fox, can tolerate comparatively little warmth, unlike some other orphans of the woodland. He observed that Snoopy frequently lay in the sun very close to a shaded area, so that

Ginger and the raccoon are friends.

Raccoon.

when he began to pant with warmth he need roll only a little way to be in the shade. During the seasons when the house had to be heated, the raccoon often began to pant, and Carl immediately put him outside where he would be more comfortable.

Throughout his relatively short life, Snoopy continued to be a beloved member of the Marty family, coming and going as he pleased, sometimes staying away for weeks, but always returning. On one such trip away from the house, however, he was unwise enough to become entangled with a porcupine either by design or by accident, with the result that he came in filled with quills. Carl attempted to remove the quills, but this was so painful for Snoopy that he ran away, back into the woods.

Carl knew that any hurt animal will make its way to water. Three days later, Snoopy was found at the lake's edge not far away. He was picked up and brought to the house, obviously a sick raccoon. Though Snoopy had managed to pull out all the quills in his body, he had been unable to dislodge those in his mouth. These had festered but could now be easily removed by Carl. But it was too late. Snoopy drank a little warm milk, then stood up on his hind legs, whining, and fell dead.

Far more unusual a pet than a raccoon is a wolf. Perhaps more misinformation about wolves has appeared in print than about any other wild animal. Wolves are invariably depicted as fierce, predatory animals, not only willing but eager to attack lone travelers. In actuality, while wolves do sometimes follow travelers(out of curiosity and always at a safe distance), accounts of men attacked by wolves are seldom authentic. Yet such legends persist, although the work of such writers as Ernest Thompson Seton and more recently Farley Mowat, should have laid to rest these and other widespread canards about wolves. Invariably, however, truth never quite catches up to fable and outright prevarication.

Northern Wisconsin is at the easternmost fringe of the natural range of the brush wolf, which is very similar in appearance to the shepherd dog.

*The raccoon
wants to eat.*

The otter plays with the raccoon.

The wolf that came to live with the Martys had been raised in Rhinelander, not many miles away. Fearful that her wolf would not survive the attacks of hunters since she was a friendly creature unused to mistreatment, her owner brought the animal to Carl. She was full-sized, weighing approximately fifty pounds when she joined the Marty family.

The wolf was welcomed, as were all animals, by Ginger, exactly as her father had welcomed the animal friends of the household before Ginger's time. Although the wolf had frequently been tied up at her first home, she was a gentle, friendly creature and was free to roam the woods at the Northernaire or make herself at home in the Marty house, where she stretched out on the floor and slept like any dog. She was the playmate even of the fawns that came to the house. Children were unafraid of her and played with her, and she was among the gentlest of the animal friends Carl Marty made.

Carl found it easier to "tame" the wolf than any fox he had had. Yet despite her friendliness, the wolf was deeply resented by some neighbors of the Northernaire who found it impossible to believe that this animal would not turn into a ravening beast as soon as opportunity presented itself. While she was in every way a highly desirable friend of the Martys and the North-

*A baby raccoon has to learn
to eat without spilling.*

The grownup raccoon eats more tidily.

ernaire guests—many, never having seen a wolf before, quite readily mistook her for a dog—other men in the vicinity of the Northernaire distrusted and even feared her.

Carl's first intimation of this came when the game warden reported a complaint that the wolf was the leader of a pack. The plaintiff was mollified when Carl and the game warden took the wolf over to him and allowed him to see for himself how tame she was. But this complaint had hardly been laid to rest when another was made, and yet another, and it became impossible to satisfy them all.

Perhaps it was inevitable that the wolf would be shot. How many times she was shot at before being hit no one could say. Certainly, before very many months passed the wolf was being persecuted, and it did not come as any surprise when she finally came to the house with a bullet lodged in her shoulder, too badly wounded to survive. The only grain of satisfaction that Carl had was the knowledge that she did not have to lie in the woods suffering for days before dying.

The wolf was far readier to extend her friendship to human beings than they were to accept it. In a real sense she was the victim of false legends about wolves—legends that Carl Marty has spent much of his life trying to dispel.

Brush wolf.

4. Tanga and Others

OF ALL THE ANIMALS to be found in the north woods of Wisconsin, the black bear is potentially the most dangerous because of his size and strength. Yet even these large and powerful animals—weighing as much as 750 pounds—are essentially peaceful, and their ferocity is invariably wholly defensive. Despite their unwarranted reputation, black bears tend to be amiable and to go about their own business without paying much attention to human beings nearby unless they are goaded to anger. Tales of pursuit by ferocious bears are complete fabrications, for no man can run fast enough to escape a bear that means to catch him; heavy as bears are and ungainly as they look, they are much faster than a human being on foot. People familiar with nature know that the traveler in the woods who tells of escaping pursuit was chased by something other than a black bear.

A bear cub, however, is an engaging and appealing creature, as are the young of all animals, and Carl Marty's first bear was four months old when the game warden brought her to the house near the Northernaire. She was

First meeting of a two-week-old fawn and a two-year-old bear.

so lacking in aggressiveness that at her first sight of a fawn she took her thirty-five pounds off up a tree in great haste to escape the seven-pound fawn, and it took her a week to get used to the delicate creature. Even then, although she was no longer afraid of the fawn, she never came closer than ten feet.

She did not have a similar fear of people, perhaps equating every human being with Carl, who fed and cared for her. She permitted herself to be carried and soon had the freedom not only of the house and grounds, but also of the Northernaire. This had to be curtailed when she began to explore the guest rooms, since by this time she was a full-grown bear, and guests were wholly uninformed about her gentleness.

Adopting an almost full-grown bear, however, was a somewhat different experience. The bear came to Carl when she was already completely grown. She had been raised by local people unable to trust wild animals to the extent of letting them have full freedom and had been kept chained to a ring in the floor every night. The people who had raised her had named her Tanga, and they assured Carl that she had come to accept being chained to the floor at night.

The bear cub has ambitions.

Somewhat dubiously, and against his instinct, Carl did chain her to a ring in the floor the first night, since she had been brought in during the early evening and he had not yet had time to make her acquaintance. Perhaps she sensed in Carl a new kind of friend, for she immediately protested. The moment the chain was snapped to the ring, she took hold of the chain and began to pull, bulging the floor boards.

Carl unfastened the chain at once. Thereupon Tanga paced all around the room, familiarizing herself with everything in it. Then she ambled out into the kitchen where she found the door, opened it, and went outside. Carl made no attempt to change her mind; he had learned from long experience that when an animal has made a decision no amount of force will change it, and with an animal as large and powerful as a bear, even to try was courting danger. Instead, Carl snatched up some sugar and hastened after her to walk at her side. He knew that any bear's favorite food is sugar (given a choice between honey and sugar, a bear will take sugar every time). Tanga had no objection to his company, and together they walked down the road until finally, some distance from the house, Carl offered her the sugar in his hand. After she had eaten it, she turned and walked back to the house with him quite docilely, doubtless seeing Carl not only as her new "owner," but also as the purveyor of the sugar she liked so much.

Once in the house, she began to satisfy her curiosity about her new home. Almost immediately she found the ladder to the open-deck attic and climbed up. In the attic she came upon all manner of stored things and began to throw down everything that came to her paws—deer antlers, Christmas tree ornaments, a chest full of blankets—everything within reach. After virtually emptying the attic, Tanga came back down and resumed her exploration of the house, passing from room to room until, having finally grown tired of her examination, she stretched out across the foot of Carl's bed.

But Carl wished to have the bear's full confidence. He crossed to the bed, sat down next to her, and gently stroked her fur. Tanga indicated neither pleasure nor displeasure at this; so Carl ventured to bare his forearm and extend it toward her. At this point Tanga could have thrust his arm away with some damage to it, or she could have responded in friendly fashion. Carl was taking a calculated risk, but he was confident that the

An unusual picture of bear and otter.

bear would respond with friendship. His confidence was not misplaced. Tanga took the skin of his forearm between her lips and foreteeth and began to purr, presently relinquished his arm and nuzzled it.

Curious to see what the bear would do if she found herself with a companion, Carl got into his pajamas and slipped into the bed, where he had to lie on his right side in an exaggerated fetal position, since Tanga was now asleep across the foot of the bed and he did not wish to disturb her by thrusting his feet under her. In that position he fell asleep and slept until a weight on his shoulder woke him.

He found Tanga lying beside him, her head on the pillow and her arm on his shoulder. Since there was more danger of being scratched while Tanga was asleep, Carl rolled over on his stomach, cradling his face in the crook of his arm so that it would not be exposed to any aimless movements on the part of the sleeping bear. But since Tanga lay quiet and unmoving, Carl presently dozed off again to sleep for several hours before he was awakened once more, as dawn approached, feeling an oppressive weight on him.

This time Tanga was on top of him, with her paws against his cheekbone. Carl was concerned for the first time, but he was still confident that by lying still he would escape any unintended injury. Once again his confidence was justified, for in a short time Tanga rolled over and lay again with one arm on his shoulder.

At last Carl slipped out of bed and curled up on the davenport for the remainder of the night; he had achieved a rare feat in sleeping next to an unchained bear on an acquaintance of less than three hours, and again proved to his satisfaction the docility of the animal.

In the morning, refreshed by her first rest free of a binding chain, Tanga celebrated by tearing up a large part of the linoleum on the kitchen floor of the Marty house. She then left for the woods, from which she came back from time to time to visit.

But Tanga was not yet done with examining her new surroundings. Several nights later a telephone call summoned Carl to the Showboat, where Tanga was reported on the top of the nearby recreation building, busily tearing off shingles. Carl went over at once. Tanga was straddling the peak of the roof and with singular deliberation tearing off one shingle after another and sailing each one through the air. She seemed to be enjoying herself, so Carl left her and took up his usual evening place at the door of the Showboat, where he was in the habit of greeting guests.

In a little while Tanga climbed down from the roof and came over to the Showboat. For a time she paced back and forth in front of the building, but soon she came up to it and peered in, then opened the door and walked in. A show was in progress, and the spotlight picked out Tanga and followed her. Untroubled by the light and unconcerned by the people, the bear skirted the guests at the bar and made for the theater lounge, while Carl took the microphone to warn guests—much more accustomed to the occasional inquiring visits of deer—to remain quiet and on no account startle Tanga by any sudden noise or movement.

Tanga mounted the stage and took her stand beside the vocalist, Rose Marie Bell, who sang her number without showing any qualms she might have felt. The song finished, Tanga moved offstage and walked among the tables circling the stage. Most of the tables were occupied, but Tanga found a vacant seat near the show's magician, Kismet, who offered her a drink after she had sat down. She was not interested in anything but satisfying

Two otters playing with a bear cub.

her curiosity, however, and in a short time she climbed down, went for a brief run around the bar, and finally made her way out of the Showboat. She climbed back onto the recreation building roof, tore off a few more shingles, and then returned to the woods.

Her brief orgy of destructive exploration over, Tanga settled down to become an amiable creature in her visits to the Marty house. She was too mature to take any pleasure in playing with Ginger or the other smaller animals, but she molested nothing and no one, coming and going as she liked. Inevitably, she remained away for longer and longer periods.

The youngest bear ever brought to Carl weighed only fifteen ounces. Its mother had been shot while hibernating, and the little bear was brought to Carl inside a hunter's jacket. Since the February weather was very cold, the cub already had pneumonia when it was brought in. Carl did his best to save its life, but the cub died in two days, in spite of Rusty's mothering.

Cub triplets brought in later were considerably more hardy, weighing approximately ten pounds each. Their mother had been caught in a wolf trap and killed, and they were discovered high in an aspen tree nearby. The tree was chopped down and the cubs escaped, but they tried to follow their dead mother as she was being dragged out of the woods and so were

Ginger and the otter.

captured. The game warden brought them to Carl. The month was April and the weather was still cool; keeping them adequately warm was the immediate problem.

Carl wrapped them in a blanket and placed them not far from his bed on the sleeping porch. He had not been long in bed, however, before one of the cubs climbed up the foot of the bed and got in with him. The other two followed in short order. If they had remained close to his body, Carl would not have objected to their company; but the cubs insistently crowded up to lie across his face, presumably for the warmth of his breath.

He returned them to the blanket, but they climbed into his bed once again. Next he moved an armchair close enough to the bed so that he could stretch his own arm onto it. At first the bears tried to walk up to Carl's face, but eventually they stayed in the armchair, all crowding up to his arm. So they spent the night, and Carl's stiff arm and neck next day were a reminder of his nocturnal companions.

The little cubs were extremely active and moved about constantly by day. They were particularly fond of boxing, standing up on their hind legs and jabbing at one another for minutes at a time. They were also interested in exploring their surroundings and quickly discovered that a portion of the porch screen, well up from the floor and seemingly beyond their reach, was weak and broken. During their second night they tore away a larger portion of the screen at that place and made their escape.

The following afternoon they were discovered in a treetop in the woods and captured once again. This time they were brought back to Carl in a stout wooden cage. Carl was dubious about keeping them there; he was against any kind of cage on principle, and he was not at all sure, in spite of the game warden's assurances, that the wooden cage would hold the cubs.

The three cubs were deceptively peaceful in their quarters, as if to lull Carl into believing in their acceptance of the new situation. But by two o'clock next morning, when Carl went to look at them, they had chewed their way out of their wooden cage, through boards only a trifle less than an inch thick, and again made their way from the house by way of the screen.

This time they made good their escape. All along Carl had thought them able to take care of themselves; this was proved when from time to time during the following months they were reported as having been seen together in the extensive woodlands of the area, never far away from the Northernaire.

Ginger and the otter in the snow.

On one occasion an adult bear afforded guests at the Northernaire, and Carl himself, something wholly unusual in instructive entertainment. Carl was summoned one afternoon from his house by urgent word from the Northernaire that a bear was trying to break into one of the rear doors of the hotel. Carl hastened over and found a large black bear tearing away at the door, while guests inside were attempting to hold it shut. Since this could have been dangerous for them, Carl immediately asked them to step back, and opened the door for the bear.

Possibly lured by tempting fragrances from the Northernaire's kitchen, which was too far from her point of entry for her to find, the bear came into the hotel and blundered up the stairs after trying in vain to open a closet door. Upstairs the bear found a bed and lay down to sleep for a quarter of an hour.

Carl remained nearby, and at the end of her nap persuaded the bear to come downstairs and out of doors once more. Among the guests at the hotel at that time was Irene Castle, famed dancer and equally famed protectress of helpless animals, for whom she built a "castle" known as

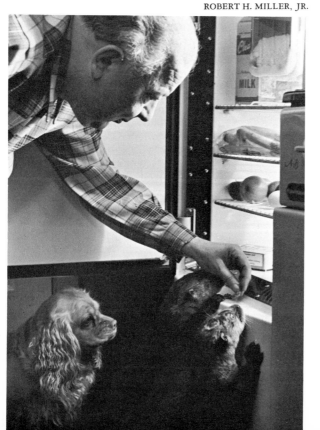

The otters hunt supper in the refrigerator while Ginger looks on.

An otter rings his special doorbell and Ginger answers.

"Orphans of the Storm." Mrs. Castle watched Carl with the bear and impulsively decided to wrestle with her.

Carl attempted to dissuade her, but without effect. Mrs. Castle advanced upon the bear and proceeded to wrestle with her for several minutes, until the bear took her arm in her mouth and held it. Mrs. Castle was too wise to attempt to pull her arm away, but left it in the bear's mouth until the arm was released unscathed. Despite the fact that adult bears customarily are not much given to play, Mrs. Castle proved by her daring that in some circumstances adult bears will play.

Invariably, the younger the animal, the more playful it is, and to some extent it is true that the smaller an animal is, relatively speaking, the more playful it remains after reaching its adult size. Certainly no more playful animal than the otter exists, as Carl Marty and many another lover of animals who has ever known this attractive creature can testify. Ernest Thompson Seton has rightfully called the otter "the noblest little soul that ever went four-footed through the woods."

Otters joined the circle of Carl Marty's wilderness orphans almost from the beginning. The dependence of the young and the friendly curiosity of the adult win friends for the otter. They made themselves at home at the Marty house with simple ease, exploring every nook and cranny of it and every gadget in the building. They accepted Carl's proffered friendship even to the point of taking food from his lips. Once introduced to the Marty household and once having known Carl's hospitality and the dogs' reciprocal playfulness, the otters were in and out of the house like members of the family, which indeed they were.

The river otter, indigenous to all parts of the United States except the far Southwest, is perhaps the most naturally playful of all animals and continues his playful habits throughout his life. Not a hibernating animal, he is active in all seasons, but retiring by nature, and so is infrequently seen except by travelers in the wilderness familiar with his ways and signs. The most characteristic signs are the otter slides—well-worn stream-side declivities down which otters slide playfully into the water, only to come galloping up the slope for another slide. This kind of play occupies them for surprisingly long periods of time.

Despite his reputation as a notorious fish-eater, the otter eats very little fish, and then commonly nongame fish—the coarser, slower-moving fishes

An otter playing in the house.

One of the otters playing in Deer Lake.

that are easier to catch. It prefers turtles, shellfish, frogs, salamanders, worms, insects, and snakes. Since he devours large numbers of fishegg-eaters, he is a vastly beneficial animal which should always be protected.

Otters reared in captivity make perhaps more affectionate pets than any other wild animal. Moreover, the animal's grace, playfulness, and natural intelligence endear him to his human friends. Carl Marty's otters were no exception. "There is surely nothing that walks on four feet that is greater than this little animal," concluded Carl after his friendship with otters began. In curiosity and dexterity the otter ranks with the raccoon, which has an advantage over the otter in the extreme flexibility of its paws; in all else the otter is superior. Perhaps more than anything else, the quality of the otter as an individual, added to his usefulness, prompted Carl to begin a campaign for his permanent protection from trapping and other hunting in Wisconsin.

The otter is also a skilled fighter, but fights only in self-defense. Pound for pound, however, another water dweller is the scrappiest fighter in the wild—the muskrat. Since he has more enemies than most animals and must live in dread of fluctuations in the water level which may flood or strand his house, the muskrat tends to be difficult to approach and wary in his habits. Yet Carl was able to pet his first muskrat within five hours of acquiring it.

The muskrat was brought to him in winter, when everything was frozen over. Although muskrats are active throughout the year, their winter pattern is well established, centering about their houses, from which they range to hunt food. Carl's muskrat had no other house but the Marty house, so Carl kept him in the bathtub, from which he moved about the house as he liked. But he was rather more solitary than other animals Carl had befriended, for one day he left the bathtub and went into the utility room, from which he could not be coaxed out. He had had a nail keg for a home in the bathtub, but evidently found the greater darkness of the utility room more to his liking. He emerged from it from time to time to get an apple or other food to eat, but he cunningly avoided a box trap Carl set for him in the hope of returning him to the nail keg in the bathtub. The muskrat is primarily a vegetarian and prefers to feed on the stems and fleshy parts of plants, but since it was winter, Carl had little of his favorite food with which to tempt him.

Eventually, however, the muskrat was set free. Thereafter at his own whim and discretion, he joined the other animals at the Marty home and in the animal house. He proved tractable and pleasant with his fellow animals and did not object to occasional bedfellows such as beavers and raccoons.

Not even the skunk is likely to be as determinedly individualistic as the muskrat. Carl has had somewhat less experience with skunks than with

Otters playing on the lawn at Bear Point.

other animals. It took an unpleasant drenching to teach him that skunks are as reluctant to use their principal weapon—the nauseating liquid they discharge from their scent glands—as venomous snakes are to loose their poison. Misled by legends about skunks, Carl made an attempt to pick up a skunk along the highway one night by the method suggested by the legend-spreaders—by the tail. His next experience with a skunk was considerably more cautious, and his first approach to him was made through Ginger.

The skunk had come to eat the food at the animal house, having discovered, in the course of its customary night wandering in the woods, the well-marked trail other animals had left leading to the house. Seeing him there, Carl picked up Ginger and carried the dog outside where she could see the skunk. Only when the two animals were aware of each other did Carl put the dog down and urge Ginger to approach the skunk very slowly, as she had been trained to do, stopping each time the skunk indicated alarm. At Ginger's approach, the skunk stopped feeding and raised up, but since the dog immediately froze, the skunk resumed eating.

In this fashion dog and skunk came together and soon were eating side by side, neither one troubled by the other. It was the same with every other skunk that came to eat, and none ever again had occasion to use his odiferous weapon against Carl or the dogs. Skunks did not frequent the Marty house by choice, however, although they permitted themselves to be picked up and carried, not only by Carl, but by guests at the Northernaire. They associated freely and impartially with foxes, deer, beavers, and various other animals at feeding time, for the skunk, secure in the effectiveness of his weapon, is absolutely without fear of any other animal.

Carl found too that the skunk is an immaculately clean animal, and he had reason to believe that the protective scent was no more pleasant to the skunk himself than to the animals at which it was directed. Above all, he learned that the skunk is a much maligned animal—maligned out of ignorance rather than malice. Unlike other animals, who cunningly avoid giving away their presence, the skunk goes about his business without concern, so that while people in the wilderness are not often aware of the presence of other wild animals, they do frequently encounter skunks. In their sudden senseless shock and fright they never wait to see how strictly the skunk minds his own business, but retreat with imagination feeding

A friendly fox and skunk meet in the woods.

their fears, ultimately giving accounts of their adventurous escape from the skunk's potent weapon. Such stories add immeasurably to the undeserved reputation of the animal.

Another much aligned and persecuted animal that Carl Marty found to be not only playful but affectionate is the porcupine. This quilled rodent (there are as many as 30,000 quills on a porcupine) performs a forest-thinning service in wilderness areas and for this is often destroyed. He tends to be solitary for much of his life, but is active throughout the year. He is a predominantly nocturnal animal, although Carl's porcupine friends moved about freely inside and outside the house at all hours of the day or night.

Carl's first porcupine was brought to him only three hours after birth; he had been taken from his mother by a jack-knife operation after she had been killed. The only way to feed him at first was by means of an eye-dropper, from which Carl patiently gave him milk. Later he took milk and bread—a food liked by all the animals at the Northernaire—as well as prunes, apples, twigs, and soda crackers. Indeed, as he grew, the porcupine showed a very marked preference for soda crackers. The porcupine's craving for salt is well known, but while Carl's porcupines were all extremely fond of soda crackers and even ate axe handles into which human perspiration, had soaked, none of them would eat raw salt.

Among the most persistent legends about porcupines, Carl found, the most frequently repeated was untrue: a porcupine cannot throw its quills, although when alarmed, the animal is in the habit of turning his back toward the source of real or imagined peril, erecting his quills, and swinging his tail against anything that touches it, embedding his quills in that object. Once embedded, the quills are extremely painful. Because they are barbed, they are difficult to remove, and if not removed will fester and can cause death. Most animals can manage to remove quills from most parts of their bodies, as Carl found by experience with a deer and bears which had gotten quills into their flesh. It is much more difficult for human beings to remove quills from animals, for the animal is aware primarily of the pain, and, legends notwithstanding, usually does not understand that the human being is trying to help.

Carl also found porcupines to be extremely affectionate. One became so attached to Ginger that he insisted upon chewing the dog's fur; the same

*Carl Marty introduces
skunk and fawn.*

animal mouthed Carl's earlobe. The porcupines also enjoyed sparring with one another and entertained any audience at such boxing matches with victory dances—the winner of the match dancing around by himself as if to celebrate his feat.

One young porcupine Carl raised responded to an audience by increased activity, quite as if he understood that something was expected of him. Left to his own devices he customarily remained motionless most of the time until impelled to hunt food.

Another of the Northernaire porcupines made a guest appearance on a Chicago television station, but few animals left the hotel area, for such traveling does not fit into Carl Marty's concept of animal-human friendship. Nor are the animals at the Northernaire there for the planned entertainment of guests; they are a part of the setting and are seen only at their own inclination, not at the wish of Carl Marty or anyone else.

Ginger with two fox kits and a baby otter.

5. For Animal Welfare

AMONG THE ACCOMMODATIONS for the animals which Carl Marty built, nothing was and is as popular as the animal house in the woods, also referred to as "Ginger's House"—ostensibly a house in which Ginger can entertain her animal friends. The animal house was built on the lake shore across the grounds from the Northernaire and the Marty house—not so far into the woods as to be invisible, nor too far from the woods. Guests at the Northernaire who are interested in seeing more than the deer salt licks on the lawns can from time to time observe wild animals coming to the house for food.

The wooden house is sturdily built and has a large picture window and a usually open door. A hole in the floor accommodates animals that prefer to enter by that means, and the house is rudimentarily furnished with a davenport and chairs. Food is left there for the various animals, and they soon develop fairly regular eating hours—principally, as with most wild animals, at twilight or at night.

Since all Carl Marty's animals are orphans, the transition from looking on the den as home to regarding the animal house as home (since it is certainly the source of food) is readily made. Animal young, too, use the house virtually as a playpen. Porcupines, raccoons, foxes, even on occasion a bear, tumble and play and finally sleep together in the animal house. And as each animal grows older and spends more and more time in the woods, his return to the house at regular intervals invariably brings other animals too—animals that have not had any previous relationship with the Martys.

Adult animals follow an almost unvaried pattern in their visits to the house. The beavers customarily come first. The beaver in the wilderness usually emerges from his den at or just after sundown, swims to his favorite stand of aspen, birch, or willow trees, cuts down a slender sapling, sections it, and proceeds to devour the bark so quickly that his teeth seem to function like a saw while his paws turn the limb or section of bole. At the Northernaire's animal house the source of food is the board laid out for him, and the beaver does not take time to cut down a sapling when he needs only enter the animal house to eat. There he satisfies his hearty appetite with chopped beef, two sliced apples, four slices of bread, a dozen prunes, and some dried apricots. After such a feast he may curl up for a brief siesta, or play with a piece of rug before he leaves again for the lake.

He is followed either by foxes or raccoons. The raccoons have sweet rolls soaked in milk waiting for them, and the porcupines that come after them find a meal of soda crackers. Occasionally a skunk finds its way into the animal house, eats what it wants, and departs. At the very edge of darkness come the deer to eat apples and grapes placed where they can get at them more readily than some of the other animals.

A half mile or so down the highway from the Northernaire, on the other side of the lake, Carl Marty acquired a roadside restaurant called Chicken in the Woods. It is literally in the woods, surrounded on all sides by thickly grown woodland. Since it is not a large building, it has an air of intimacy

Carl Marty with Rusty, a wolf cub, a fawn, a porcupine, and a red fox kit.

GRANT HALLIDAY

denied so large a place as the Northernaire, and is frequented not only by passers-by and guests during the day, but by the Showboat's entertainers and guests after the show at night.

Just outside its windows Carl built a large feeding platform so that guests might have the advantage of seeing animals now and then in their natural state. The feeding platform is supplied by pans of food put out nightly by the chef. In the beginning, once the animals had discovered the food—first the raccoons, then skunks, then foxes—the chef lighted the feeding area and moved the food closer to the building itself. Finally came the platform —eight feet square and well lit. By this time raccoons and skunks were bringing their entire families to eat at the Chicken in the Woods.

Guests at the windows made the animals uneasy at first, but they readily accustomed themselves to being observed and finally became well adjusted to onlookers. Only the foxes refuse to eat in the glare of the lights; they usually bound up onto the platform, snatch their food, and then retreat to the shadowy edge of the woods to eat it—still in plain sight, but out of range of the lights' glare.

In all this the entertainment of guests is secondary. Of primary importance to Carl Marty has been the instruction of people, many of whom have no other opportunity to see wild animals in their natural habitat. They learn to enjoy seeing them and to appreciate them; and they often are disabused of erroneous notions they may have had about them.

After raising at least ten animals a year for many years and becoming acquainted with hundreds more, Carl found that anyone wishing to deal intimately with wild animals must learn certain fundamental rules. It is necessary for the human being to gain the confidence of the animal as soon as possible, and in order to accomplish this the human being must be both predictable and dependable in his behavior. There is no room for impatience in dealing with animals, nor must there ever be any effort to impede an animal's movements.

Animals respond to kind treatment in various ways. Foxes, bears, and raccoons lick hands, but beaver and porcupines will never do so. Animals

Ginger's House in the Woods in winter.

when young will respond by cuddling up to the human being, in lieu of their lost parents, and when older will tease and become playful.

The human being should always permit the animals in the wild to approach him, rather than move toward them and possibly alarm them. An alarmed animal may become defensive and ultimately ferocious. "In my experience," says Carl, "I have never seen a case of aggressive ferocity on the part of any animal. Ferocity is always defensive."

Most animals are secretive; it has been Carl's experience that far more human beings are seen by animals than the reverse. Even in the case of so large an animal as the black bear, Carl believes that for every bear seen by a human being, at least a thousand human beings have been seen by the bear.

But above everything else in dealing with wild animals, dependable kindness and affection invariably cause animals to respond in kind. This cannot be said of man.

After two decades with wild animals, Carl Marty has become, perhaps inevitably, as much propagandist as animal lover. Ultimately it is impossible to associate on terms of friendship with animals and not take up their cause against the human race, which on the whole has a sorry record in its treatment of animals, domestic as well as wild. The education by entertainment of his guests has become an integral part of the functions of the Northernaire and essentially, for Carl Marty, a more important part than any other.

Marty is not content in a passive role. Early in his acquaintance with otters, for instance, he was particularly stirred to learn from trappers that official governmental circles were responsible for the spread of harmful misinformation about these animals and, even worse, had opened the trapping season just when otters were nursing their young—from late February to early April. Perhaps the most harmful misinformation about otters was that they were habitual trout eaters, for it afforded hunters and trappers more incentive to kill these handsome and useful animals. Carl Marty's knowledge of otters told him this was untrue. The source of the misinformation—as well as the authority for the trapping season—was the Wisconsin Game Division, which made recommendations on the otter season to the Wisconsin Conservation Commission.

At the end of the trapping season in 1954 Carl met with three other men all vitally interested in otters: Emil Liers, perhaps one of the world's lead-

Bernese playing at the lakeside with a fawn and three otters.

ing authorities on otters and author of several books about them; Paul Munninghoff, a trapper operating in the Minnesota-Wisconsin region; and Walt Goldsworthy, an ardent naturalist, feature writer, and newspaper columnist. In an effort to extend greater protection to otters, the four men prepared a lengthy taped discussion of the problem for presentation to the authorities.

The conference was intended to bring out the salient facts these men had learned from actually dealing with otters. The food of otters was the first subject under discussion.

"I had the mistaken notion that otters fed on fish," said Liers, speaking of his initial experience in raising otters, "so I fed them fish, and lo and behold! I found that a steady fish diet caused a kind of anemia and then paralysis. Every pound of raw fish you feed an otter uses 3,000 units of vitamin B_1, taking it out of the system."

Carl agreed from his own experience that the major portion of an otter's diet was not fish.

Liers noted, "Anyone who observes otters closely will find that otters will not stay in an area where there aren't a lot of crawfish. Ninety percent of their food is crawfish, which eat fish eggs and young spawn. I have that on record on film."

Munninghoff added that in regard to the otter's feeding habits in the Wisconsin River, more sluggish than the creeks and rivers of northern Wisconsin, such fish as the otter took were "invariably redhorse, other suckers, and bullheads."

Carl Marty put it succinctly by pointing out that "Only twenty percent of the fish otters eat are game fish—and fish is a small part of an otter's diet. To maintain otherwise is vicious, unfair propaganda. We see magazine covers showing otters with trout in their jaws. Purely imaginary. For every trout an otter may eat, he saves fifty to a hundred."

"I'd say more than that," said Liers. "I've had as many as sixteen otters on heavily stocked trout streams. So far, they've caught only three trout, and one of these was sick. Another was in shallow water, too shallow for it to

Triplet orphaned fawns gather around Carl Marty and otter.

Ginger with a curious fawn and two friendly raccoons.

get away. Trout are simply too fast for otters. We sometimes read that people have found trout 'scales' in otter droppings. Since when does a trout have 'scales?' Game wardens have followed me on my rounds and have never seen an otter catch a trout."

Munninghoff added, "The only practical way to come to any conclusion about otter forage is by examining droppings. Fish scales are invariably those of redhorse suckers, and there are sometimes bullhead spines. There is no evidence of others. The principal food is crawfish."

"At the University of Minnesota the stomachs of fifty otters were examined," put in Liers. "Only a trace of trout was found, and these otters were from heavily-stocked trout streams. These may have been the remains of sick or disabled trout."

The unanimity of these four men, all of whom were familiar with the

Orphan fawn nibbles the ear of singer Lois Marker.

otter in its natural habitat, was not shaken by a single disagreement on the issue of the otter's feeding pattern. The same agreement attended the discussion of the breeding and whelping habits of the animal.

Carl Marty opened with the statistics on the otter taken during the trapping season—the end of the period of gestation: "Six hundred otters on the average are taken in a season between February and early April, when the majority of otters are born. For every nursing otter taken, two little otters are left to starve."

"I've never had an otter born later than March—some as early as January or February—but never later than March," said Liers. But the Wisconsin Game Division held that March was not the whelping month of otters, despite the evidence of these capable authorities.

"In my experience, an otter breeds again immediately after whelping," said Carl. "The gestation period of an otter is from ten to twelve and a half months. The latter may be delayed gestation. Otters don't begin to breed until the second year."

The Game Division also maintained that otters were caught primarily in beaver sets, to which Munninghoff, an experienced trapper, took swift exception: "Out of a thousand otters taken, only three were caught in beaver sets—three-tenths of one percent."

"We contend," said Carl, "that the Conservation Commission is acting on mistaken and misleading information. We believe that trappers know that otters are not taken in beaver traps except incidentally, and we don't know on whose mistaken information the Conservation Commission is acting to mislead the public. We are concerned that all the facts be analyzed and passed upon. This does not seem to have been done."

The experience of trappers in the Three Lakes area confirmed the findings of this panel. The results obtained by protecting otters in countries abroad added weight to those findings—the excellent fishing in England, where every five miles of stream, according to Liers, has an otter and where salmon have increased eight-fold in otter-protected streams, as in many other parts of the world where otters are protected.

On the evidence presented, Oneida County closed the otter-trapping season, although the goal pursued by Carl was the permanent closure maintained in some foreign countries (notably Switzerland, where both otters and fish abound). In the area immediately adjacent to Three Lakes and its

A badger has come to play with Ginger.

The badger rolls on the floor in play.

chain of lakes around the Northernaire, Carl had traveled by boat 11,500 miles in two years and never seen an otter—the result of trapping in the nursing season. Research in countries where the otter is free from trapping has shown that the otter actually aids in game management by preying on such rough fish as suckers. But systematic trapping of otters has continued in Wisconsin, to the detriment of game fish in the state's streams. The elimination of such a natural enemy as the otter has allowed fish-egg eating predators like turtles, crawfish, and snakes to multiply and diminish the fish population.

Although the facts laid before the Wisconsin Conservation Commission effected the immediate closing of the otter trapping season for a year in Wisconsin, in the final analysis the Commission did not retreat from its original position, which was in effect a denial of the humane aspect of the problem. The Commission's argument was simply that trapping bred otters resulted in as great a loss of the animals as did the trapping of nursing mother otters. The Conservation Commission, in short, was still far behind the game-management practices of foreign governments, which demonstrates anew that the struggle to make widely known the potential of animal friendship for human beings faces tremendous odds.

Two otters inspecting a camera.

ROBERT H. MILLER, JR.

Afterword

WITH A QUARTER of a century of animal friendships behind him, Carl Marty today can look to some lasting results in his campaign for understanding wilderness dwellers. His efforts and those of his friends have brought about the closure of approximately twenty-five thousand acres to hunting, a protected area sizable enough to assure the safety of many animals who will probably not wander beyond its boundaries in their lifetimes. The inevitable poachers are still to be found, but such depredations by the human animal have never equalled the slaughter during the regular hunting season.

88

Bernese, a fox, and a fawn at their games.

Singer Dorothy Ferguson feeds the otters.

Doe at the Northernaire in winter.

Bernese supervises two fox kits.

Carl Marty's attitude toward animals has spread throughout the Three Lakes area and beyond. The northern Wisconsin woodlands have become increasingly attractive for retirement, not only for their great natural beauty, but also for the immediacy of nature in the presence of animals who seem not to fear man because of the friendship of men like Carl Marty. Feeding stations are now widespread in the area, developing friendly relationships between human beings and the animals of the wilderness.

However slowly and against however great odds, Carl Marty's philosophy is taking root and spreading from the Northernaire. Certainly Carl Marty has gone far more than his share of the way to win and hold the friendship of animals, of whom he has said, with profound truth, "Relatively, it is not the animals that are wild, but the human beings."

*A badger follows Ginger and
Carl Marty out of the woods.*